SAMMY'S TREE-MENDOUS

Christmas Adventure

W9-CBV-025

It all started because . . .

I am a shepherd boy. I spend most of my time out in the hills taking care of my sheep. Sometimes I get lonely because I have no one to talk with.

One of the lambs, Sammy, seems to understand my loneliness. He stays close beside me, and I talk to him as a friend. Now I know that Sammy doesn't really understand what I tell him, but he listens so closely that sometimes I wonder . . .

Lately I have been telling Sammy about Christmas. It makes me feel a little less lonely when I remember the special things my family does together at this time of year. We have so much fun shopping for gifts, decorating our Christmas tree, baking Christmas cookies, and going caroling!

Of course, there is more to Christmas than that. I tell Sammy that Christmas is the special time when we celebrate the birth of God's Son, Jesus. There are some wonderful Bible stories about the birth of Jesus. Sammy loves to hear them. He seems to imagine that he is right there in the middle of the action.

How about if I tell you how my family celebrates Jesus' birthday? I'll also tell you some stories from the Bible about the first Christmas. See if you can find Sammy and me in the pictures that follow. While you are looking, try to find the crazy things shown at the bottom of each page. If you get really good, look for the ones listed at the back of the book!

Illustrated by
Daniel J. Hochstatter

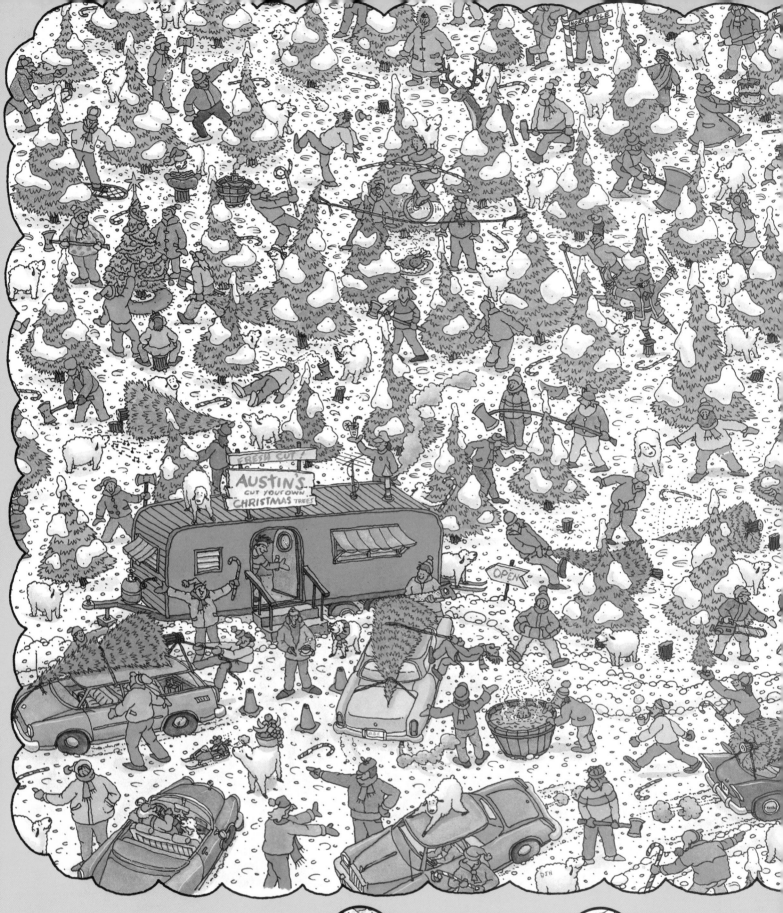

Roller Stroller

Spaghetti and Meatballs

Better Duck

Blowing Bubbles

LOOKING FOR THE PERFECT TREE

Every December we remember the wonderful birth of Jesus. We celebrate in special ways that have become traditions we enjoy every year.

One Christmas tradition in my family is to put up a Christmas tree in our home. We have lots of fun looking for our tree. We bundle up in warm clothes, and we go out to the forest. We look and look, hoping to find just the right evergreen tree. It has to be the right height, with nice full branches.

When we find the one we want, Dad and I cut it down and tie it to the roof of the car. We take it home and put it in a special Christmas tree stand in our house. Then Mom serves us hot chocolate with marshmallows!

Broken Handle

Snowmobile Mouse

Biker

Sherlock Sheep

Holiday Hideout

Soldier Sheep

GOING CHRISTMAS SHOPPING

Another holiday tradition is going Christmas shopping at the mall. The stores are brightly decorated, with displays of things for shoppers to buy. Christmas carols play over the loudspeakers, and many people hum or sing along. In the center of the mall stands a huge Christmas tree.

The stores are crowded with holiday shoppers, but we look through every store for that special gift for each person on our lists. I feel good when I find a gift I know someone will enjoy. Giving gifts to family and friends is a nice way to tell them how special they are to us.

 Nice Catch

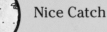 Moo Moo

Soprano Sheep

Army Aimer

Ewe-nicycle

Lemonade Sipper

DECORATING THE TREE

After the Christmas tree is up, Mom brings out boxes of ornaments, tinsel, and lights. My sister makes popcorn, and we string the popcorn and some cranberries to make a long garland.

Then we decorate our Christmas tree. We all take turns putting on the ornaments and arranging them in just the right positions. Many of the ornaments hold special memories of the people who gave them to us. Others we made when we were little.

When all the ornaments are in place, Dad lifts my little brother up high, and he puts the shiny star on top of the tree. Then we turn out all the lights in the room, and Dad turns on the tree lights. Our Christmas tree is so beautiful, we just sit and look at it together.

Sleepwalker

I Got It!

John Dough

Blindfolded Baker

Calling for Cookies

Twin Topper

MAKING CHRISTMAS COOKIES

One of my favorite holiday traditions is making Christmas cookies. All the kids help. One measures the flour. Another cracks open the eggs. Someone else mixes the dough and rolls it out on the counter. Sometimes we are a little messy, but Mom doesn't seem to mind!

We use cookie cutters in the shapes of Christmas symbols such as stars and angels. After the cookies are baked, we decorate them with different colors of frosting and sprinkle them with colored sugar.

We wrap some cookies in colorful cellophane and tie pretty bows on top. Then we take them to our neighbors. We get to keep the rest! Cookies you have made yourself really taste great!

Cat in the Box

Doughy Dozer

Fruitful Woman

Spaghetti Eater

Balanced Mouse

Mama Bear

THE SCHOOL PROGRAM

For weeks before Christmas, we practice our school program. The actors and singers study their parts. We all learn Christmas songs and plan where to stand and what movements to make. The teachers paint scenery and build props. Our moms or grandmothers sew our costumes.

Finally the big day arrives. We all gather backstage, dressed in our costumes and jumpy with excitement. Our parents fill the auditorium and hope that their children remember their parts.

Then the program begins. In word and song, we tell the story of the birth of Jesus and the joy of Christmas. Cameras flash and video cameras whir as proud parents record the program. When the program ends, we all laugh and hug one another. It has been a good day!

Hothead

Please Pass the Potatoes

 Melon Heads

 Carpet Ride

 Hot Dog Dinner

 Lovely Lamb

THE TRIP TO BETHLEHEM

Mary and Joseph were expecting their first baby very soon. He was going to be a special baby. Angels had told Mary and Joseph that He was the Son of God. His name would be Jesus, and Mary and Joseph had been chosen to be His earthly parents.

But right now, Mary and Joseph were on their way to Bethlehem. The ruler of their land wanted to know how many people lived in his country. So the people had to go to their family's hometown to be counted. Mary rode on a donkey, and Joseph walked with her as they made the long trip to Bethlehem.

Rodeo Rodent

Belinda Ballerina

 Seed Shooter

 Head Banger

Fruitful Woman

Long Beard

NO ROOM AT THE INN

Mary was going to have her baby any day now, and Joseph was worried about her. They had traveled a long time to get to Bethlehem, and Mary was tired.

Joseph stopped at an inn and asked for a room where they could rest. But the innkeeper did not have any empty rooms. In fact, he told them that there were no empty rooms in the whole town! Bethlehem was crowded with people who had come to be counted in the census.

The innkeeper offered to let Mary and Joseph stay in the stable where the animals were kept. At least they could sleep on the soft hay. So Mary and Joseph settled down for the night in the stable, surrounded by gentle animals.

Alarm Clock Smasher

Count Sheep to Sleep

 Love at First Sight

 Police Catching Picker

 Hot Dog War

 Relaxed Rodent

SHEPHERDS SEE ANGELS

A flock of sheep grazed quietly on a hill outside of Bethlehem. The shepherds were relaxing by the camp fire. It had been a busy day, and they were enjoying this quiet time.

Suddenly an angel appeared in the sky. "Do not be afraid," the angel said. "For there is born to you this day in the city of David a Savior, who is Christ the Lord. . . . You will find a Babe wrapped in swaddling cloths, lying in a manger."

Then hundreds of angels filled the sky and sang, "Glory to God in the highest, and on earth peace, goodwill toward men!" The angels left as quickly as they had appeared. The shepherds hurried to Bethlehem to see the wonderful new baby!

Pig in the Mud

Hot Turkey

 Nosy Fish

 Sharp Dressed She

 Hot Coffee

 Donkey Detective

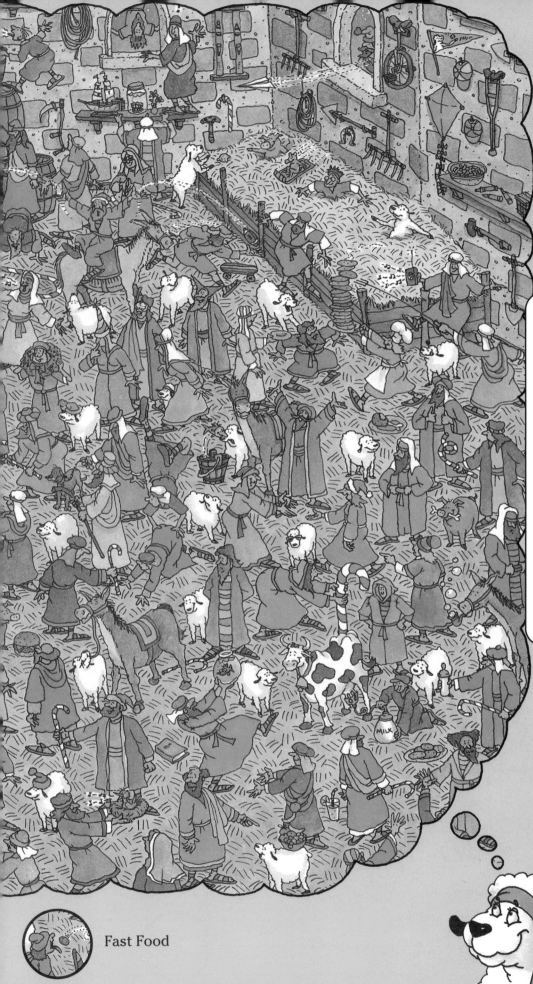

THE BIRTH OF JESUS

Mary and Joseph were resting in the stable when Mary's baby was born. Mary and Joseph named their son Jesus, as the angel had told them to.

They wrapped Him in strips of cloth, called swaddling cloths, and laid Him in a manger to sleep. A manger is a trough that holds the animals' food.

The shepherds who had seen the angels hurried into the stable. They knew that this baby was the Son of God, so they worshiped Him and thanked God for sending Him to earth.

Fast Food

Surfer Mouse

Grape Grabber

Bucky Beaver

Paper Dolls

Field Phone

THE WISE MEN VISIT

About the time Jesus was born in Bethlehem, an unusual thing happened in a country to the east. A new star appeared in the sky. It was bigger and brighter than the other stars.

Some wise men in that country saw the star and knew that something special had happened. From studying the Scriptures, they knew it meant that God's Son had been born. These wise men decided to follow the star and see where it led them. They traveled for nearly two years, following the star as it moved a little each day.

Finally they arrived at the home of Mary and Joseph. They worshiped little Jesus and gave Him wonderful gifts of gold, frankincense, and myrrh.

Doughnut Head

Underdressed

Marvelous Mustache

Mouse-tronaut

Singing Salmon

Hot Breath

CHRISTMAS CAROLING

I love to go caroling with a group of my friends at Christmas. We dress in warm clothes and walk around the neighborhood, stopping at different houses to sing Christmas carols. We do not always sound great, but we sing with all our hearts.

Some people ask for their favorites, such as "Joy to the World" and "Silent Night." We especially like to sing for people who are older or sick and cannot get out of their houses very often. They really appreciate our music.

By the time we finish caroling, we are very cold. So we go back to someone's house and drink hot chocolate and have a lot of fun!

Downhood Skier

Singing Too Loud

Wrong Reflection

Punching Present

Sleepwalker

Alphabet Soup

WRAPPING CHRISTMAS GIFTS

When our Christmas shopping is all finished, we bring our purchases home. Now comes the hard part—keeping each gift a secret. We want everyone to be surprised when the gifts are opened on Christmas morning. First we get out the colorful wrapping paper. Then we measure it, cut it, fold it around the package, and tape it. We decorate each package with pretty bows and ribbons.

Finally, on a little card, we write whom the gift is for and whom it is from. After that, we pile all the presents under the Christmas tree. But we must wait until Christmas to open them!

Dart Ducker

Behind Bars

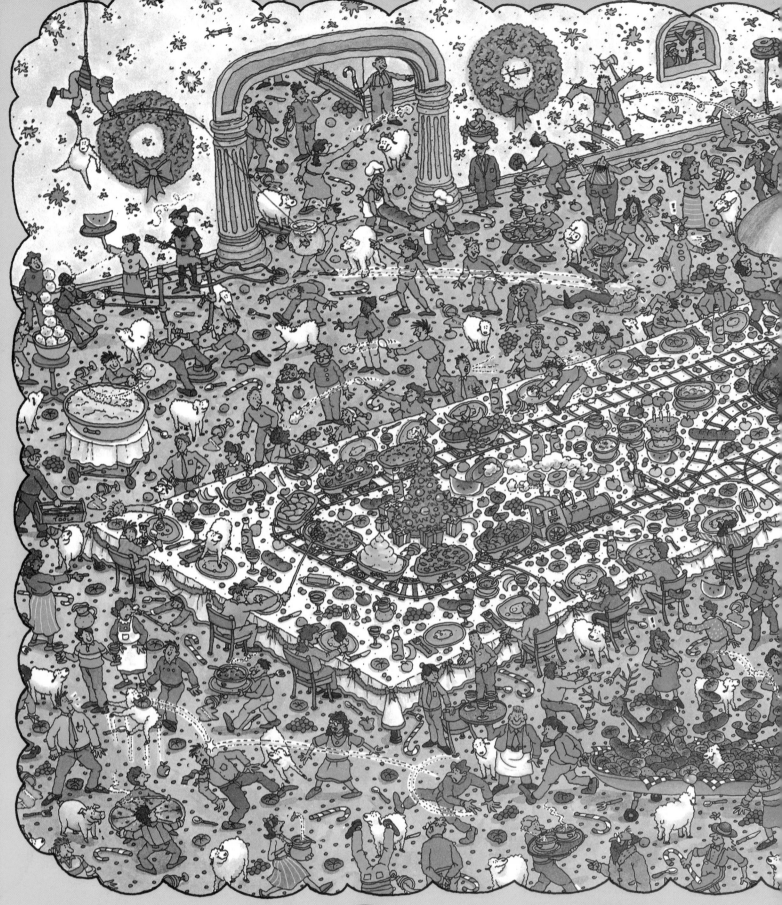

Fish out of Water

Bounced Biscuit

Do Not Bug Robin

Mad Marvin

CHRISTMAS DINNER

The best part of Christmastime is Christmas Day. We open all our presents and nibble on candy. When the smell of roast turkey fills the house, we start thinking about the wonderful dinner we will enjoy later.

Grandparents, aunts, uncles, cousins, and friends fill the house. Everyone helps get the dinner ready. Some cook and some decorate the dinner table. The kids set the table and fold fancy napkins.

Soon we all gather around the table. Dad or Grandpa prays, thanking God for this wonderful time of year when our family can all be together for the holiday. I am so thankful that Jesus was born and that we can celebrate His birth.

All Tied Up

Soup for Two

Titles
in
A Seeking Sammy Book
series:

•*Sammy's Fantastic Journeys
with the
Early Heroes of the Bible*

•*Sammy's Incredible Travels
with
Jesus and His Friends*

•*Sammy's Excellent
Real-Life Adventures*

•*Sammy's Tree-Mendous
Christmas Adventure*